THE PORTAGE POETRY SERIES

Series Titles

Talking Diamonds (2nd edition)
Linda Nemec Foster

The Green Vault Heist
David Salner

There is a Corner of Someplace Else
Camden Michael Jones

Everything Waits
Jonathan Graham

We Are Reckless
Christy Prahl

Always a Body
Molly Fuller

Bowed As If Laden With Snow
Megan Wildhood

Silent Letter
Gail Hanlon

New Wilderness
Jenifer DeBellis

Fulgurite
Catherine Kyle

The Body Is Burden and Delight
Sharon White

Bone Country
Linda Nemec Foster

Not Just the Fire
R.B. Simon

Monarch
Heather Bourbeau

"It turns out that nothing is merely ordinary. Simply to wake up to another day is already extraordinary, if we have the eyes to see. Linda Nemec Foster certainly has the eyes that are always ready for miracles, and the words with which to describe them. Through her, we see that life is indeed a glorious burden—with equal emphasis on 'burden' and 'glorious.'"

—Oriana Ivy
from her review in *Writing the Polish Diaspora*

"[Foster's] works here are exceptional and gleaming, serving as a reminder that even experts can excel beyond their own greatness."

—*The Grand Rapids Press*

"Where else should the miraculous happen but in everyday lives, in moments when humans are graced with the extraordinary through enhanced perception. Foster seems to invite readers 'come on, come on, dive in,' into *Talking Diamonds* and into life."

— Jeanne Lesinski
from her review in *360 Main Street*

Talking Diamonds

Linda Nemec Foster

CORNERSTONE PRESS
UNIVERSITY OF WISCONSIN-STEVENS POINT

Cornerstone Press, Stevens Point, Wisconsin 54481
Copyright © 2023 Linda Nemec Foster
www.uwsp.edu/cornerstone

Printed in the United States of America by
Point Print and Design Studio, Stevens Point, Wisconsin

Library of Congress Control Number: 2009924365
ISBN: 978-1-960329-11-0 (2nd Ed. Pbk)

First Edition originally published by New Issues Press, 2009.

Cornerstone Press titles are produced in courses and internships offered by the
Department of English at the University of Wisconsin–Stevens Point.

DIRECTOR & PUBLISHER
Dr. Ross K. Tangedal

EXECUTIVE EDITORS
Jeff Snowbarger, Freesia McKee

EDITORIAL DIRECTOR
Ellie Atkinson

SENIOR EDITOR
Brett Hill, Grace Dahl

PRESS STAFF
Carolyn Czerwinski, Sophie McPherson, Natalie Reiter, Ava Willett

for Rebecca

Also by Linda Nemec Foster:

Bone Country
The Blue Divide
The Lake Michigan Mermaid
  (with Anne-Marie Oomen and artist Meridith Ridl)
The Elusive Heroine: My Daughter Lost in Magritte
Ten Songs from Bulgaria
Amber Necklace from Gdańsk
Listen to the Landscape
Contemplating the Heavens
Living in the Fire Nest
Trying to Balance the Heart
A Modern Fairy Tale: The Baba Yaga Poems
A History of the Body: Prose Poems

Contents

Skin would be the same as water,
would be the same as sky—
and you were dealing mostly
in dark and light; not so much
in flesh and blood.

—Diane Arbus

A Note from the Author

For any poet and writer, to complete a manuscript of new work is a cause for celebration. To get that manuscript accepted by an amazing press (given the highly competitive nature of the publishing industry) only accentuates the great celebratory vibe. That was my experience when William Olsen, the editor of New Issues Press, accepted my full-length collection of poems, *Talking Diamonds*, for publication in 2008. The book was published in the fall of 2009, nominated for a number of book awards, and was a finalist for *ForeWord Magazine*'s Book of the Year in Poetry. I was so grateful to Bill and his staff at Western Michigan University for bringing *Talking Diamonds* into the world.

That being said, you can imagine my sadness when New Issues closed its doors due to challenging economic circumstances in June 2023. *Huffington Post* described the press as having "the best qualities of the publishing tradition." Words of praise indeed. And with those words, you can also imagine my celebratory vibe when another fine and amazing university press offered to assume the editorial responsibilities of keeping *Talking Diamonds* in print and in distribution worldwide. Cornerstone Press, sponsored by the University of Wisconsin–Stevens Point, was that amazing press. I am very grateful to Dr. Ross K. Tangedal, Director and Publisher, for accepting *Talking Diamonds* (for a second time) and keeping it alive in the world.

What you're now holding in your hands is the second edition—another reincarnation, if you will—of *Talking Diamonds*. All the poems are here along with the fine blurbs from Lisel Mueller, Sydney Lea, and Stuart Dybek—and excerpts from wonderful reviews by Oriana Ivy, Jeanne Lesinski, and *The Grand Rapids Press*. I'm so pleased this book is still walking in the world and continuing to "deepen, console, surprise" (to quote from Dybek's blurb). Again, my deep gratitude to Dr. Tangedal and the entire editorial team at Cornerstone Press. Long live poetry and its readers.

Linda Nemec Foster
Grand Rapids, Michigan
October, 2023

I.

The Field Behind the Dying Father's House

I'm the thin yellow
that escapes the dry grass,
the left-over dream
haunting the afternoon.
I'm the stillness of goldenrod
in the ordinary day
before the storm cloud breaks
and the wide trees embrace
their shadows. I possess no gift
of perspective that will deceive your eye.
I am simple and flat, a reflection
of sun forgotten on the ground.
Hovering between the earth and sky,
I belong to neither: no green
can swallow me, no blue
can overwhelm my singular purpose.
I hold this fragile landscape together
until night falls and turns everything—
the luminous barn, the brooding
house—into a quiet symphony of black.
I know its slow melody by heart.

In the Vicinity of Orion's Arm

Like the star beaming outward past its death . . .
—Robert Wrigley

Every day we die
a little more.
My young son
doesn't believe me;
with the telescope
he got for Christmas
he points to the stars,
unfailing lights of the past,
as examples of how difficult
it is to kill anything.
Infinity has not yet
begun to trouble him.
As if Pascal's true
fear of the eternal
silence of the heavens
was all a hoax.

How can I tell him
he's wrong. That death
is one theory of celestial
movement. And there
is no other. That what
we see in the sky
are ghost images:
the moon a blank
mirror, the galaxy
an open wound,
the universe a thin
veil of dust hiding
the empty mind of God.

I only know what
I know. How the universe
looks the same in every
direction. Layered petals
of rose or bleeding
womb. I only know
this night in late
January, sub-zero
temperatures, his
father positioning
a telescope in the frozen
snow of the backyard.
As if he could count
the endless blur of stars.
Imagining the faces
of everyone he's ever
loved who has died.

Alone

She doesn't know where anything is anymore;
has had to move from a huge house
on the lake to a one-bedroom condo
in the city, but she still can't find
her shoes. The black suede pumps and faux
leather boots elude her. Only sandals grace
her feet, the one part of her body
the husband never noticed. But now,
she tries to notice everything: the declension
of autumn with its homeless leaves; how small
her hands have become in the course of a year;
the sunset out her bedroom window—a ritual
as predictable as brushing her hair. "What a glorious
burden," she says to the living room wall
filled with blank space and its quiet aftermath.

Sleeping in a Room Filled with the Past

—for Arlene

How carefully you've collected your life.
A shadowbox filled with shells arranged
to resemble your mother's fine outline.

> *Staircase Abalone, Sunburst Star Turban, Cinnabar*
> *Limpet, King Midas's Slit Shell, Queen Tegula and*
> *her golden inner ear.*

Your father's here, too. Not just his ghost,
but him living in the poem you wrote
and framed on the wall above my head.

> *Clear Sundial, Zebra Periwinkle, Bleeding Tooth*
> *Nerite, Common Janthina, Violet Spider Conch,*
> *and its purple loops trailing away.*

I count no less than three small mirrors encrusted
with coral, nineteen lithographs of flowers and
landscapes at various stages of blossom and reticence.

> *Starry Moon Shell, Grinning Tun, Swollen Fig,*
> *the curled embryo of Baby's Ear Moon,*
> *the braided arrogance of Trumpet Triton.*

You own a collage of Key West sunsets, a Florentine
girl alive in sepia and white, Van Gogh's languid
sunflowers in a vase too small to embrace them.

> *Purple Dye Murex, Atlantic Distorsio,*
> *Eye-of-Judas Rock, the raised leg*
> *of Pavlova Typhis, the menacing Venus Comb.*

Cheap imitations of the Eiffel Tower and Pisa's lean;
the wall continues to hold France—some elegant
Riviera town. A kite floats away, no hand in sight.

> *Spiral Babylon, Many-Ribbed Neptune, Catalina*
> *Forreria, Spiral Melongena, quiet longing*
> *of the Blood-Stained Dove Shell.*

Too many pink and red-striped Cheshire cats,
too many dancing clowns, the Virgin Mary
in a holy card in the bottom of the top drawer.

> *Queen Verillum, Armoured Vase, Perverse*
> *Whelk, Twisted Dwarf, the hesitant*
> *gesture of the Unapproachable Pagoda.*

A shock of recognition: a picture by my daughter
when color mattered and nothing else. Not the perspective
of the table falling forward, not the reality of still life.

> *Linda's Morum, Dubious Volute, Tiger Auger,*
> *Queen Marginella, the Japanese Wonder Shell,*
> *pale fortune cookie that inspires architects.*

But her sense of the magenta of the air,
the chartreuse of the ground, the insistent
pink of an awkward fork extending like compromise.

> *Pearl Ammonite, Green-Lined Paper Bubble,*
> *Umbrella Shell, Stiff Pen crusted into*
> *the golden fleece, Hooded Ark's brittle star.*

Extending like a lost hand beyond this room filled
with pictures of brothers, sisters, grown children,
and the ex-husband no one talks about.

Pacific Lion's Paw, Boar's Tusk, Lazarus
Jewel Box, True Heart, and the Dilated
False Angel Wing as blue and dim as Paris.

The past lives you've survived and left behind:
background, black; glass frame, broken.
The braided cord of your necklace heavy with pearls.

I Enter My Mother's Dementia,

and she lets me in:
calls me
"Irene" (her sister)
and "Maryanne" (her mother)
or at times
just "Mom" or "Mama."

> *Thank you for the flowers, Mom.*
> My mother says to me, her daughter.

And I don't fight the inevitable,
her mistakes.

> *Pearls melt in vinegar,*
> she calmly states. I nod.

Don't correct her like I did
when she was young and coherent,
bitter and mean, married to The Wrong
Man. She'd proclaim this phrase
as if it was a movie title and she,
the unfortunate heroine in the starring
role. Olivia de Havilland trapped
in a private elevator. *Lady in a Cage*
played out in the Cleveland suburbs.
My father was no Clark Gable, no
Jimmy Stewart. Not even Errol Flynn
on a good day. The marriage, A Big Mistake,
another fake title from a borrowed movie.

> I find an old letter that she wrote
> in 1974, the year I married.
> "OK. You better pay that wedding dress
> yours self. I hate that dress, OK?

Don't do nothun for you. Looks like
hostess gown, hostess gown that hostess
wears in restaurant like Brown Derby
or that Italian place on the West Side.
OK? You pay all yours self. You should
buy that nice dress at Ann's Vogue Shoppe
on Broadway with the lace and ribbons.
OK? But no. You buy that ugly dress
that don't do nothun for you. You will
look ugly and skinny bride. OK?
I don't know why he marries you."

Your Mom

I don't correct her grammar,
spelling, or punctuation.
But I keep the letter, a souvenir,
a third-class relic from an erstwhile
saint: Saint Helen of the Spotless
Bathroom, Saint Helen of the Worn
Rosary Beads, Saint Helen the Housewife.

Attention, attention, Mom, she says
to me. *Happy Birthday, Merry Christmas,
Happy Easter, Happy Anniversary, Happy,
Happy, Everything. Because they work
it that way, they work it that way.*

As if every holiday had an agenda.

I've heard the family rumors:
my mother consulted gypsies
who read tea leaves. Made sure
every dark stain of tea
was invoked three times before
she let her body conceive me
on the night of her thirtieth birthday.

When I was born, the moon
was waxing gibbous: swollen,
pregnant, humpbacked, silver disk
not quite fully illuminated.

> *You don't know what nothing is.*
> *When I was your age, my father died.*
> *Never cried at his funeral neither.*
> *No time, no time. Then five years later,*
> *my mother died. Again, no tears.*
> *You know why? I didn't want to do*
> *nothing after that. Not even cry.*
> *What's the use? The dead can't hear it.*
> *But me, I heard my mother calling*
> *my name every day long after*
> *we buried her. Early in the morning*
> *before I woke, late in the evening*
> *before my dreams carried me*
> *across the night's river. Always*
> *the same voice from that dark place.*
> *'Helen, Helen.' Her voice so clear*
> *as if she was in the basement*
> *calling me down to help her fold*
> *clean, white sheets.*

Skin flawless, pure alabaster. No scar,
hardly a wrinkle, amazing for a woman
orphaned at 15. "Like pearls," I hear
myself say in spite of myself.
She loved them. I never did.
That's one of the things that was wrong
with my wedding dress. Not enough pearls.

I prefer amber. So much history to wear
around my neck, my wrists, piercing
the flesh of my earlobes. The ancients

had it right: the Greeks knew
amber was the only organic gemstone;
seemed to hold light at its very core
so they called it "elektron"—
substance of the sun. The Vikings
believed amber symbolized the tears
of the goddess of love. The Chinese
tell the story that when tigers die,
their souls become amber. And in Poland,
amber is known as gold of the sea.
Poland—the wounded heart of Europe—
that created my mother and father
in its tight embrace.

I imagine a cluster of amber
growing around a woman's neck
as she listens to a polonaise.
The music mixing with the slight
breeze that touches the roses
in the garden behind Chopin's house.
She is not my mother.

        Vincent van Gogh
        Vincent van Gogh
        Vincent van Gogh
        My mother mumbles to the wall,
        this woman who has never
        set foot in an art museum,
        emphatic about the Dutch painter
        being as omnipresent as television.

Later I swear I hear the same phrase
and it has nothing to do with art
and everything to do with TV news.

        Events and guns, events and guns,
        events and guns,
        and my quiet, almost closed ears.

Piano Recital: Sonata with Mother and Child

—after Rilke

The young girl in white sitting
in front of the massive black piano
is not intimidated by Mozart's
allegro assai; even when her fingers
falter and her hands' collective memory
forgets its past, or more importantly,
its future. The keys become deep
snow, stark black trees. She tries
to grasp the thin branches, to imagine
their lace pattern against the blue dusk.
Each second of silence beats louder than
her heart, the muffled metronome in her chest.

In the back of the concert hall, the mother
can do nothing but close her eyes, hold
her breath, and pray that her daughter's
fingers abandon the snow and trees
and embrace the abstract landscape
of no color, pure wind, rush of cloud birth.

The Shape of Rain

The shape of rain has nothing
to do with the shape of clouds,
those faces we imagine in the sky.

The shape of rain has everything
to do with the shape of our hands;
but we forget the rumor of this.

The shape of rain is not the opaque
veil of life. Not the dancer's robe
in a fairy tale on the verge of being spoken.

The shape of rain is the wide, clear
curve of suicide. Bright and empty
concave of silence. No echo of regret.

The shape of rain looks straight down,
the long leap that sifts through miles
of dead air to reach the glory of pavement.

9-11-01

—*for Clarence Major*

You said there is no present.
We only have the past and
the future because the now
is so minute, so finite,
it's over before it's
begun. But we are doomed
to live in the present.
And when I think of your words
now, today, when time stopped
and was turned upside down,
the hourglass retreating
into its own amnesia
of disbelief, the day
that burned the present
in our minds, the plane
captured on video, hitting
the South Tower again and again.
As if time lost all sense
of itself and forgot
to move forward, a man
caught in thick fog
arguing with himself
over what day it is.

Tonight, No One is Safe

I.

The young mother in suburbia
locked in a brick house
is awakened at 2 A.M.
by a man who isn't
her husband. He rapes her
in bed, drags her down to
the basement, rapes her again,
and stabs her once in the arm,
as if to say: *I didn't mean it.*

She is almost grateful
her husband is out-of-town,
snoring in some motel room
in Toledo, dreaming of the next
morning's business deal. Grateful
her two sons sleep through it
as the intruder ties her up and
drives off with the family van.

Police are telling everyone
in the neighborhood to keep
everything locked, to keep lights
on at night. Weeks go by,
with no arrest.

The woman across the street
calls me to say she can't
sleep. She sits by her lighted
window. Watches the empty street.

II.

We try to pay attention to the music.
Rodrigo's guitar concerto can almost
take us to Madrid and the hidden
breeze that weaves through the deserted
garden of Aranjuez. Only trees live
there now. And the hands of the guitarist
perfecting blossoms of veronica
and jasmine: smell of crushed
hyacinths; jagged eye of the moon.

But in the deep pause that shapes
everything we hear, we begin
to believe the myth. How the strings
of the first guitar were made quietly,
simply, from a drowned girl's black hair.

Modern Landscape: Two Views of the World

I am the dream of water
the parched land begs for
each night. Small drops
of crystal that glow
like the moon. I am the wind
that carries this dream
from village to village,
house to house, from mother
to mother. I am the brown
that covers their tight skin,
and the burnt orange hair
of their fragile daughters.
I am the thin line
of gray that begins
another day: again.

I am the dream of air:
invisible and bored.
The transparent glue
that holds a city together.
I am the blue sapphire piercing
a pale woman's ear
and the millennia of grief
that put it there. I am
the small explosions of lightning,
brave troops of fireflies
transforming the meager
backyard. I am the one
question that keeps the lonely
man awake as his dead
father peels away the night.

Copper Harbor: Early October

Smell of memory and regret and we expect
each leaf, without hesitation,
to engulf itself in its own quiet fire:
the maple turning from light green
to crimson; the oak turning from dark green
to russet. We assume the days grow shorter
and they do, as if to please us, their shadows
lengthening into the forests of pine.

And in the open meadows and low swamps,
the rocky shorelines and wet woods, we know
every wildflower signals its own death—
white of the virgin's bower and boneset,
yellow of the tansy and spotted jewelweed,
red of the Indian paintbrush and cardinal-flower,
purple of the loosestrife and nightshade,
blue of the skullcap and closed gentian,
green of the ragweed and wormwood—
all their colors will effortlessly change
to vague gray before the deep cold begins.

Look at this landscape, the place
that takes nothing for granted.
The sun rises like a sleepy, swollen eye,
while mallards write an uneven calligraphy
on the lake with the short, dark strokes
of their bodies. For them, migration
is calculated chaos: how to get from
point A to point B without dying.

And look at us, with our intense observations,
as if we were spectators that really mattered.

We witness the brief high-color season
when even the weeds enter a state
of self-realization and it stuns us. The hope
that at the end—at the very moment we leave
all that we have become to enter
the coldest of seasons—our colors will be true.

Total Eclipse

It's not that the moon gradually leaves us,
changing its white sound of lullaby
to the hollow silence of shadow.

Or that it slips from being innocent bystander
to the fleeing criminal stained blood-red
barely visible in its transparent disguise.

It's not that the tides become despondent
for lack of direction, a clear signal
they can plot their monotony by.

Or that every tale about the moon's
gleaming face is a lie, a mere pretense
to calm us into accepting night.

It's not that the moon even returns
like an errant child who pretends
to run away and then disowns the threat.

It's this: the moon can leave and come back
to still find us with our whole bodies intact,
unchanged; except for our deaths, a little closer.

II.

Birth

—for Jeanette

Today I spent all afternoon with an old friend.
We talked about how difficult it is to hold
a life in your own two hands, as if you
could embrace an echo. Later the conversation
shifted to dreams: hers filled with spiritual
resonance—having lunch with the Dalai Lama
in her suburban kitchen; mine weighted
with twentieth-century absurdities—Aunt Irene's
house transformed into a bowling alley for poets.

In mid-sentence, my friend is startled by a moth
the color of dusk. The dark wings seem to flutter
right out of her shoulder. If we were in a dream,
she whispers, this small act of flight
would be a good sign. Tonight, I cannot sleep.
Instead, I watch the heavy rain change
into a fine mist that astonishes even the sky.

Vision

—for Terry Blackhawk

This is the part of your life
you're not prepared for:
a tropical beach, Diamond Head
in the distance as predictable
as a cliché, a postcard back home
on your refrigerator in Detroit.
Your husband and son are out there
somewhere, splashing in the Pacific.
The salt water buoying up
their bodies like holy levitation.

But you—afraid of water—an anomaly
in this place, this chain of islands
surrounded by nothing but. Your pale
skin on this tanned beach screams out
haole—Hawaiian for ghost,
walking dead, body without breath.

So nothing prepares you for this vision:
Our Lady of Guadalupe on Waikiki.
A blue ocean away from where she
first appeared to that dirt-poor
Indian peasant on Tepeyac Hill,
you can't miss her shape of glorious
color coming towards you: deep teal,
bright vermilion, bronzed gold tattooed
on the chest of a huge Mexican from Baja.
Even his back is emblazoned with her back
and you're stunned by the accuracy
of detail; the little angel at her feet
holding a sliver of the crescent moon
as if she were a living, breathing icon.

No, a holy card like the one you
always wanted in fourth grade. And not
just any holy card of any common saint:
Agnes with her lamb, Jerome with his lion,
Lucy with her eyes on a plate,
Thomas with his doubt. But the Mother of God
in all her human manifestations.

Mirror of Justice,
Seat of Wisdom,
Vessel of Honor,
Mystical Rose,
Tower of David,
Tower of Ivory,
House of Gold,
Gate of Heaven,
Star of the Ocean.

This ocean, this beach at your feet
as if she were Botticelli's Venus
washed ashore with the sea foam,
washed ashore for your approval.
And you tell yourself this isn't a miracle,
only a tattoo; this isn't anything
extraordinary, only your life,
the crowded beach, the husband and son
waving impatiently for you to just
come on, come on, dive in.

The Third Secret of Fatima

She knows it has nothing to do with the end
of the world. Angels blowing trumpets. Plaster statues
of the Virgin weeping salt tears. Whore of Babylon,
dressed in purple and scarlet, alone in the desert.

Nothing to do with the number of days left
to us: as unreliable as the number of rooms
in heaven. Or the color of their walls, or if
they have windows facing west. She's convinced

that the secret is ordinary. Like something in her life
she's forgotten. The exact architecture of her face
as she fades into sleep. Whether or not she is happy.
As she plants the garden, still no clue. Only

dirt; a disconcerting sense of growth where she
least expects it. At the edge of the garden,
her daughter appears almost unnoticed. She
holds a fist of wildflowers. She wears her mother's face.

The Blind and the Lame Swim at the "Y"

For one hour they can lose
their bodies in the water
and become seamless veils,
long cascades of movement.
The drooling girl with large
breasts cuts through her laps:
a shining line of quicksilver
even her own mother doesn't
recognize. The blind boy opens
his white eyes underwater
and with their fluid paleness
reflects trapped rainbows.
But it's the crippled girl
with a slash for a mouth
that amazes the water. Tiny
deformed feet that curl
like tender shells forgotten
on some deserted beach,
become the shining, sleek fins
of a mermaid's tail. The water
embraces her as if embracing
one of its own: a wave, seafoam,
the broken sun that falls
on the surface of the ocean.

But this is not the ocean.
Only a quiet afternoon in a town
where soon the children will return
to the estranged bodies they left
at the water's edge: breathing life
into twisted feet, blind eyes,
the raw breasts no man will touch.

Then their mothers will know them.
How they hum to themselves, rocking
back and forth, fingering their silent
places. And their mothers will welcome
them without regret, without regret.

Because the secret heart of every
fairy tale is locked deep within
these children. Because this heart
beats in goodness which is rarer
than perfection. Because this heart
is like the water: uncaring yet
kind, transparent yet full.

Paranoia for Two Voices

A boy goes into respiratory arrest

   a woman forgets how to play the piano

the father makes a killing on the stock market

   and a UFO hovers in the backyard

he has dear friends he never talks to

   an imaginary juggler trying to hold the stars

but stays up all night reading junk mail

   the answer is here somewhere

and even the Dalai Lama cannot know

   but only the dying man in his white room

how the secret lover who works the midnight shift

   understands the foreign agent

who touches all her mail

   who reads poems and faints

believes sex begins and ends

   on the other side of the world

in the same small-fisted stone

   which tries to tear itself apart

where nothing happens twice

   unless (of course) it does

Parasailing Above the Pacific

For one long moment you lose yourself:
become air, the clear wind
above the volcanic jaw of Opunohu Bay.
You forget the tense job on the other side
of the world, the dying mother, wayward son.
Even the thin plastic line, the blue tether
connecting you like an umbilicus to the boat
300 feet below, can seem to blur
into the rush of sky. How amazed
you are by your lack of fear—you, the one
scared of heights. For one long moment,
total silence surrounds you. And in that moment
you understand the wisdom of rain: the way
it disappears so completely into the ocean
and becomes a seamless veil around purple
coral, the scattered diamonds the sun
discovers below your dangling feet.

Her Obsession with Older Men

When did it start? When she was
30, 35, 40? No, it was 45—
that pivotal age when she
was beyond life's mid-point,
almost out-of-control. The boredom
of 45 and knowing it. The knowledge
that maybe the young boys
have been left behind for good
with their acne and egos
still tangled-up in tight jeans
and styling gel. But to have
an older man, and not just any,
but *the* older man. Foreign,
but not too exotic—like England.
Yes, the safety of understanding
his language even though
it sounds different. And he
wouldn't have to be as old as
her father but only as old as
a very, very young friend
of her father's. Tall and graying
and elegant. And they'd have
to have nothing, nothing in common.
In other words, not Cockney
but Etonian. *Brideshead Revisited*
not *EastEnders*. He would have
arrogant gestures, arrogant nostrils,
and an almost furtive disdain for sex
until she seduces him and makes him
screw her in her dreams. His body
connecting with a wildness that can
only be attributed to Druids. And

she notices every inch of his body,
every nuance: the discreet
diamond in his left earlobe,
how his mouth groans in orgasm,
how his cock finds the perfect
spot inside her. Only his chest
remains a mystery. It hides
in the shadow of dark hair
but then becomes the paradox of roses
tattooed on his white, white English
skin. The roses climb his pale
chest. Petals, stems, buds, thorns—
all entwined with the dark coils
of his hair, pulling her closer.
And hidden behind the hair and roses,
his heart beats steady. Every beat
making him another second, another
minute, another hour older, older,
older. She presses her ear against
the roses and listens. Listens.

A Sign from God

*. . . a 20-pound carp about to be slaughtered . . . began
speaking in Hebrew, shouting apocalyptic warnings . . .*
—*The New York Times*, March 15, 2003

Now, anything is possible.
Next thing you'll tell me
your dead father speaks
to you through the distinct growl
of your dog, Stafford. And there's
the clumber spaniel now at the back door
channeling not the famous poet
but Dad, the famous basketball coach:
barking out positions in the locker room,
howling pleasure (or disgust) from the sidelines.
You swear it's him—back from the dead—
but you look down from your morning coffee
and see only the family dog staring
at you with half-open eyes, salivating tongue,
wagging tail. "Dad, Dad," you almost say
knowing in your head he's not there
panting away on the kitchen floor. But
in your heart, you want him to be.

To be—like the miracle in New York—
thirty miles from Manhattan. The talking carp
pleading for his life in a Kosher fish market
ready to be gunked on the head
and made into gefilte fish for Sabbath dinner.
Pleading for his life in Hebrew (what else?)
shouting: "*Tzaruch shemirah, hasof bah.*"
Translation: "Get your act together and repent
because the end is near."

And it's not as if the fish is channeling
the troubled soul of a dead rabbi. Or that
the two fish-cutters at the New Square Fish Market
are holy men ready to hear the word of God:
one, a devout Gentile; the other,
a middle-aged Hasid with one wife and eleven kids.

It's only that you want to believe the dead
will live again. In the open mouth
of a 20-pound carp, in the soft breath
of your klutzy pooch. The voice of your father
as quirky and ominous as the voice of God.
Telling you to plant the garden now—
now—before the clouds change colors. Before
it's time for dinner in the evening,
the walk in the morning. Now—
before you start to fade like rain
evaporating off patio furniture, like dusk
dissolving into night, abandoned attics,
empty garages. Before you forget the small
movements a mouth makes as it forms
each word around the quiet air.

The Tao of Junk Mail

Like a paper flood with nowhere to go
it patiently rises an inch every day:

piles in the kitchen, piles on the sofa,
piles at the foot of your unmade bed

next to your shoes. How personal
it gets—smelling the remnants

of your smelly feet—calling you
by your first name. "Linda, Linda

open me first. I need you,
I need you more than you

need yourself. To contribute, to join,
to save, to win, to ponder, to agree,

to decide, to buy." The well-rehearsed
litany of the trivial by-product

of civilization. For that's exactly
what it is. What happens when we exchange

our animal skins for the predictable
package of a business envelope. Bulk

mail of letter-perfect white. No smudge
of error, your name and address just right.

The Nature of the Beast

Forget the soft white fur,
gentle purring and green eyes
half-closed while the sleek
body curls around your feet.
Forget the exaggerated elegance
of the thin tail as it tries
to find the true direction of heaven.
Forget the money wasted on exotic
food: broiled artichoke hearts,
fish eggs garnished with watercress.
The collar studded with rhinestones.
The measured breathing on your bed,
your pillow; pink tongue close
to your lips. Forget the tiny diamonds
of electricity that a cat will give you
if the air is right, if your hand
strokes its body in just the right
balance of love and neglect.
Forget all of this when the cat
shows its simple, uncluttered nature
that kills a nestling, revels
in the limp body—the corpse
complete and nameless as anything
you have ever owned.

But remember how it holds the gift
tenderly in its mouth, approaching
you like a child, a lover who wants
to give you the gift of its wildness.
And remember your response. The turning
away, the walking back to your
self. That gray place of uncertain
affection, gloved hand, lonely wisdom.

Wild Pheasants in the City

Their lives were filled with irony.
The man and the woman, whose marriage
was expensive and convenient, wanted it
that way: adultery without guilt;
children without obligation; calculated
weekends in the country renting
a stranger's cottage. No matter
that they hated the country. Its clean
air and clear rivers, its infinite
rows of trees and immense night sky.

What they did trust was the irony
of the big city. The soft whir
of tires on asphalt, the deep comfort
of complete anonymity. So imagine
their non-surprise when pheasants
began to appear in their citified
backyard. First, the glittering jewel
of the male: emerald head, ruby
crest, singular ring of diamond
about the neck. Followed closely, but
not too closely, by the obligatory female:
brown, just brown, like the wet earth
after a heavy rain. How these birds
got there, looking awkward yet content
in the cramped yard, was no mystery
to either the man or the woman.
No random freak of nature.
It was irony, pure and simple.

But not the perfect irony
which solely belonged to them:
that one moment when their bodies
touched and their minds went blank;
when they forgot their names,
and their rationale of untamed things,
when even the wild birds forgot how to fly.

False Spring: After Follain

They almost believe it: this warm air caressing their faces.
The calendar with its languid rows of days whispers late
January, but the lovers have forgotten what season it is.
As if Time was willing to walk anywhere in his sad, black shoes
just for them. What they think they see is each other; what
they really see is a transfigured memory of a reclining nude.
The head erased by desire, the torso ready to be framed like
a black and white photograph. Silver nitrate so exact that
even the birds are duped. And robins take on the sleek
distance of a premature flight to view the lovers in their
public display. In their car they move dangerously closer
together, opening and closing their mouths, saying nothing,
breathing silence. In the car in front of them, a woman still
in winter sees the lovers in her rearview mirror. Two dark
shapes huddled in the small rectangle of light. Somewhere
behind the faceless clouds, the sun attempts to pantomime
its resurrection.

Late Winter

The tired snow worn-out by city dirt
hardens into gray rock. The road crews
are out, cleaning the grates and sewers
of the debris left-over from autumn,
the recent past that no one remembers:
crisp brown leaves now turned limp and black;
a torn, red glove; newspaper headlines
whose intensity is muted by the season's amnesia.

The men clean in silence, only the radio
from their pick-up truck blares the lament
of Bonnie Raitt's love letter. What they dredge up
is left behind for another crew to haul away.
As if they're allowing us one small moment
to see what runs in the dark veins
of our streets, what forgotten half-lives
sleep content under our houses while we
turn restlessly from one dream to the next.

Climbing Cherry Trees

Before you can possess them in your hand—
soft globes of perfect color—
you must climb and hang on:
become the tree scraping your knees,
the bark leaving its stigmata on your hands.
Only then will you be able to taste
the color, not just the fruit,
but the color of the fruit.
Deep red of fragile skin,
cherry red of succulent heart,
mahogany red of stained pit.
Imagine a stone of pure vermilion
dissolving in your mouth.
The color never leaving your throat
as you sit there in the embrace of the tree
not belonging to the heavens,
but not quite belonging to the earth.

Family Pose

This is my mother and my father
standing close together,
one year into their marriage.
She hides behind him,
as she hides her first pregnancy,
her face peers over his shoulder.
I am hiding inside my mother
making her large, her body
a chore to keep around.
She is embarrassed.

But both of them are laughing
as if someone told a joke.
And I am laughing too;
the small sunken teeth
hold the grin for the camera,
hold the grin tight.
You can see it in the negative:
there, the small, white light
that lives alone, that lives between
the shadows of its dark parents.

Talking Diamonds

—for Irene

Late at night, when dreams still live
inside us, you can hear a soft
noise like the quiet sound of
diamonds talking
about their lives underground.
Never are they bitter or angry. Nor do they
even curse those dark
memories of suffocating black. They know
every facet of their brilliance began as mere
coal—a mere dark fist waiting
for a chance to be something
other than ordinary.
Something hovering just under
the surface where anything and
everything can happen: talking diamonds,
rain becoming white orchids, ourselves awakening.

III.

The Skin, The Blood: The Artists' Dialogue

—after Yvette Cummings and Michael Cassidy

I.

In this small space, anything is possible.
My skin surrounds my soul like a tight
glove, black leather jacket, claustrophobic
garage. It has bumps and bruises—
brilliant scarlet, quiet magenta,
Prussian blue seeping over every pore.
I can be cut open and sewn back up,
sucker-punched and left for dead,
gravely wounded and resurrected like memory.
My skin reads like a map of personal topography—
Mountain Range as Kick-Ass Ambition,
Flat Plateau as Boring Compromise,
Tectonic Plates as Bipolar Siblings.
I dare you to touch me.

II.

How can blood touch anything but itself?
Anything but the same kaleidoscopic
patterns of blue, white, and red cells
circulating like the sun in a narrow room,
like wasted days in a week, a private
calendar filled with white boxes
and little else. My entire universe seems
shaped by the quiet sound of grief
as it reaches the heart, listens to its hollow
echo, and finally like a clean exit
wound, bids farewell, farewell, farewell.
You dare me to touch you. I dare you
to stop time for one solitary second
and see what happens: everything or nothing.

Groping

*An explosion and gas fire at a power station sent flames
and smoke hundreds of feet into the sky . . . At the
Metropolitan Museum of Art, about 20,000 people
found themselves groping in semi-darkness.*
—*Cleveland Plain Dealer,* December, 1989

Imagine them, the lovers of art,
in that half-darkness which can be
as dense as blindness, trying to find
their way among the Vermeers and the heads
of Aphrodite, the Rembrandts and the Egyptian
tomb girl, the Monets and the Byzantine mosaics.

The consuming dark closes in, pushes the art
lovers from Abstract Expressionism to Realism,
from Rococo ceilings to Renaissance portraits,
from Gothic sculpture to Ashanti fertility masks.

And still the darkness pushes them back, further
and further until they might as well be in the caves
of Lascaux, stooping to fit into themselves:
afraid to touch the walls that are damp
with the lives of animals just killed.

Village of the Mermaids: After Delvaux

I sit here with my pale sisters
and try to forget the ocean's
pull: tangled hair of purple

anemone that weaves around
my silent name; broken diamonds
of sunlight suspended in water.

We try to adjust to the monotony
of air. How its dryness
clings to our skin, our lips.

It's useless. This pretense that
life on solid ground is somehow
better. Better for what?

Rocks? Men? Houses and furniture
are boring. Efficient mausoleums
with tiny doors and beds. Chairs

don't make sense as we sit
on them like sentinels waiting
for our new feet to work.

Maybe we should comb our hair,
fold our hands, wear dresses
that cover us like wedding gowns.

Maybe we should discard the memory
of water and the sound of water,
how it filled our glad, open mouths.

Is this how the world makes us forget
our singing history and hear nothing
when the small shell is pressed to our ear?

Bad Art at the Clarkston Motor Inn

Insomnia lives here, right next
to the dust on the Gideon's Bible
forgotten in the night stand's
top drawer. So it's up till three
flicking through the static on the TV's
four channels, counting the mint
green tiles in the bathroom and
measuring the off-gray grout
that secures their universe.

Above the sink—a tiny mirror and
a tiny picture of an unmanned
sailboat floating in spite of itself
towards your reflection. And
back in the bedroom, stuck
on the wall near the closet
sits "The Old Sailor" thick
with acrylics and bad memory.
Is that a cloud or an afterthought?
How can a pipe resemble a nose?
Why does his disembodied face
loom like a storm on the horizon?

Forget him and look at what's
directly over the bed. The world's
largest pink carnations jumping out
of a too-clear glass vase. Peering
down on your sleepless head,
they could be your last chance
for a little excitement. "Looks so
real you could eat 'em," the desk
clerk told you last night, extolling
the virtues of women and art
in the same room. Wide awake,
desperate, ready for anything.

Nativity Scene Encased in Saran Wrap

—after a painting by Nancy Ann Van Pelt

The carefully arranged scene—Magi and camels,
floating angel and stunned Virgin—covered in thin plastic.

"I could tell you stories," she said. "Who's having sex
with whom and why Jesse uses men's ties to map the world."

The universe as a cardboard box, back seat of a Dodge,
motel room rented by the hour. Thin smoke leaving her lips.

In the beginning was the wordless conversation. Nothing
but syllables strung along the vast expanse of empty air.

Well, yes. Well, no. Ummmmmmm, maybe. She doesn't think
the answers strange. Only the 3 boxes filled with his coughing.

The self-taught artist never titles his pieces. "Why bother?
My art is all that mismatched stuff people throw away."

She uses cuttings of her own hair to braid a heavy
wall of dull brown. Memory, she calls it, or Names of the Lost.

"A woman who doesn't wear perfume has no future," said Paul
Valéry. Or perhaps it was his neighbor commenting on the rain.

It's all connected, she says. The full manger and abandoned
landscape. Birth and resurrection. Lilies of the field on Valium.

The Son's Dream

—after a painting by Bruce Erikson

We only see his body
strewn on the bed
as if he's ready to fall
off the mattress
out of the painting
onto the floor at my feet.

The light from an invisible
source shines on his sleeping
groin waiting for a revelation:
what color will the sky
assume tomorrow; why is his pillow
the color of the dying sun?

We can't see his dream
where his upturned face and open mouth
envision his childhood home—
white and large—with endless
hallways leading into empty rooms.
No mother in sight.
Only blank walls to greet him.

And in the backyard, in the garden
lush with green—the vegetables
of late summer, the flowers of early fall—
the son's father is working his hands
into the rich, deep, and yielding earth.

Contrapuntal: Negative Space

—after Christine Olson

The two sisters shared

                    light and shadow

a bed in that back room

                    that held secrets

cold in the winter

                    silver frost on the window

hot in the summer

                    night breeze in the curtains

they held their breaths

                    as the seasons changed

as they watched the moon

                    from their small room

rise every night

                    they escaped into each other

from the empty space between them

                    and the muted dusk

The Reinvention of Myth

—after a mixed media installation by Wilma Lok

The reinvention of myth begins with a fairy tale
about a woman from the sea,
mermaid image of flesh on water—
and a man from the sky,
blue light reflecting the clouds.
A story about how the two met
and became the horizon. Here is
their union, one thin line
bordering the world. Holding the firmament
in place. And here is a child
from this, a daughter who plays
on the beach as intently as God
creating on that first day.
Light, water, sand, and her
movements form landscapes
she will name like new constellations:
Desert Island Rising from the Ocean;
The Heart as Buried Treasure;
Earth Collected from the World's Sorrow.
The daughter will release these names
into the air like small winter birds.
And each will sing its own myth:
birth and its long journey,
death and the murmur of the sea.

Body Temple: The Teacher Addresses the Student

—after Amanda Lee

You adorn yourself with white-washed pages
of the Bible. Spirals of plaster of Paris
barely covers the words of first Kings,
second Kings, Hosea, Nehemiah.
But where are you in this House of God?
Trapped inside with no doors or windows;
your soul a collection of one-dimensional
black figures that scream and yell and
pull out their hair trying to find balance
between belief and unbelief,
the precarious cross and fertile body.

I would rather be a mermaid caught
in a transparent kayak, an icon waiting
to be worshipped. Consider my outstretched
arms, perfect breasts, the encased womb
as blueprint of your first home.
I could be the new crucifix of the new century
challenging every dogma, every catechism
you memorized to keep body and soul separate.

I am one woman trying to carve
wood into some image and likeness. I can visit
your town, your neighborhood, your street.
I can peer into your house and try to assess
the damage. Or I can continue to row
beyond the breakwater and imagine your leap
from solid ground to fluid sea. Unfettered
by bricks and mortar, theory and design,
the rhetoric of what keeps us
from ourselves and what locks us in.

Red Amaryllis, 1937

—for Larry Pike

Everyone has many associations with a flower
You . . . lean forward to smell it or maybe touch
it with your lips almost without thinking . . .

—Georgia O'Keeffe

I.

I am lost in this flower—
lost in its deep red,
its stiff and erect stamens:
vigilant soldiers guarding the center.
I am lost in its sensuous petals
as you were once lost in a woman's
open mouth, open legs, her deep
center surrounded by flesh
so pink it had to be art, you said,
painted there with soft brushstrokes
not merely created by cell growth,
boring mitosis found in some
sophomore biology text. But honest-
to-god, oil-on-canvas, glow-
in-the-dark fuchsia making labia
and clitoris brilliant and permanent.

II.

It's not a museum but a strip joint. And as we walk through
the side door, you tell me that what happens here
is the closest thing to art you can experience on the planet.
The place is dark but the black lights make your gin and tonic
glow like a radioactive night light. Not to mention the naked
women lap-dancing all night long. Perfect tits shining
with baby oil. Cunts shaved to runway strips of dyed hair.

When the girls aren't peeling their clothes off or gyrating
above the hips of some drunk whose wife is nowhere in sight,
they take over the women's room. Make-up bags heavy with gloss
and mascara, tight sequined outfits, tiny G-strings barely
there. Or they satisfy the regulars. Share jokes and small
talk. All of them are named after flowers: Violet, Lilly,
Rose, Heather. Daisy keeps combing and braiding the long hair
of a man in a wheelchair. The most tenderhearted thing,
you say, you've ever seen. But in that strip joint that night,
I saw something even more tender. When the black girl
with erect nipples came to dance inches from your face,
you stood up, took her hand, and began to waltz. Waltz—
proper and dignified—as if you two were Arthur
and Katherine Murray, as if the club's D.J. was playing
"The Blue Danube" and not a gritty, throaty "Mustang Sally."
You waltzed and she followed with her naked body. She laughed
and said she never waltzed before in her life. And every man
who saw you dance with her smiled—even the bouncer. Smiled
the smallest of smiles filled with nothing but distant memory
and faint regret. After the waltz, you kissed her hand.
She said her name was Jasmine. Flower of night air
and moonlight, you replied.

III.

The year before you died,
you inundated yourself with colors.
Not the garish neon of the strip joint,
but the brilliant palette of O'Keeffe's art,
a wall calendar.

> Unexpected scarlet of January
> White bone of February
> March and its convolution of green
> April blinded with burnt sienna
> Wild yellow song of May

Tall blue stems surrounding June
July and wave upon wave of orange
August exploding into magenta
Red opening into September
Aquamarine sky of October
November's hold on tentative mauve
December and its one note, gray

This litany of color you could recite
in your sleep, until the one night
you kept yourself awake to watch
the sun rise on an early December morning.
How you noticed every nuance of black
becoming less black, becoming gray,
becoming dull white, becoming blue.
The colors on your street finally
remembering themselves. As if you
saw it all for the first time:
the world putting on its dazzling wardrobe
and you, wanting to touch every glistening strand.

Forgotten Desire

—after a collage by Darlene Kaczmarczyk

They must have some memory of us,
those things we leave behind. The small
red petal, lost in a vase of pure crystal.
Or the black negligee that triggered lust
and then was eventually discarded just
after the husband's prolonged fall
from grace: the grace of knowing all
the intimate details of his once-beloved's face

and hair and thigh and breast and secret
places of desire. All forgotten now,
along with the lace bustier and matching thong,
the satin tap pants and black velvet
camisole. The empty shell of a low,
strapless gown. Once flowing, now gone.

Venice

—*after Yvette Cummings*

Remember me? My sweltering July
in '95 when you and your husband
melted into each other in that small
room near the train station. Leaky
faucets, smell of cat piss, broken
bottles cemented into the courtyard's
walls to keep the rest of the world out.
Every night, your sleep was interrupted
by squads of diving mosquitoes. Your husband
trying to kill each one, leaving its bloody
body on the white wall—a trophy
to take a picture of (and you did)
along with the dozens of other attractions:
the Grand Canal and its languishing gondolas,
San Marco and its dazzling mosaics,
the Bridge of Sighs and its quiet breath.

Now, your memory of me is layered
with the present, your ordinary life:
stacks of junk mail, unread newspapers,
dust collecting in every corner of the house.
How easy to forget the islands of glass
and lace blurring into the Adriatic.
How easy to forget your getting lost in my labyrinth
of alleyways, only to surrender all sense
of direction and—like the miracle of a magnificent
city built on a swamp—find your way
to your husband waiting for you at a table
in an open-air cafe in the Piazza, sitting
as casually as if he'd been there all his life.
And you, with your American sweat, finally

understanding the meaning of foreign and native,
improbable and impossible. Not quite ready
to leave the abandoned Byzantine church,
the modest park with its sleeping pensioners.
Not quite ready to leave in the dead of night
and start retracing the almost forgotten way home.

Souvenir

—after a painting by Marc Chagall

Deep scarlet of Paris
melting the Eiffel Tower
like a tourist's cliché.

Soft crimson of lovers
the splayed hand touching
the hollow of neck, matted hair.

Loud fuchsia of a boy
embracing a sheep as if the idea
of sunrise surprised him every morning.

Empty red of a man
trying to fill the vase
with fragments of memory.

The transparent woman
alone at night with the silent
moon keeping her awake.

The Gray Anatomy of the Crowd

—for M. A.

The crowd's season is always autumn.
As countless trees lose their leaves,
it loses what it never possessed:
hesitant gesture of a hand,
soft curve of a neck,
imagined contour of a face.

The crowd never notices these losses.
As inconsequential as losing
a strand of hair, a flake
of skin, the jagged edge
of a bitten fingernail. Formless
as a fog, the crowd consumes the air.

How can you count the crowd's
presence or absence? How can you
embrace the empty torso,
the vacant shell of ribcage
where the heart, that solitary
sparrow, once sang?

Holding the Air

—after an art installation by Wilma Lok

A girl flies a kite in a landscape
that could be anywhere: cold
mountain, hot desert, landlocked
prairie, tentative edges
of the sea. The air always
looks the same—transparent,
nothing to see but its breath.
And the girl with her kite
touches its invisible hand,
walks in procession with its clouds
like a sleepwalker, a nomad searching
for the next place to call home.

Here, there is no home—only the sky
reflecting what she gives it.
A tangled design of string and paper
as if trying to write her name
in a foreign language.

At night she dreams of weaving
a huge quilt filled with the patterns
of open hands: punctuation of black,
question of why, answer of the wind.

Deserted Fairground, 1947

—after a painting by Ben Shahn

*"a metaphor for the solitary aspect
of human existence . . ."*

—gallery notes

You wanted to paint this metaphor:
grass as mere stipple of lines, empty tents
as hollow extensions of themselves. Their perspective
awkward like the broken spokes of a discarded umbrella.
Could this be how you imagined the Sinai desert—
forty years of tents and the Jews still wandering
under a sky of dirty white and quiet mauve,
no end in sight? Where is the hand of God
in the emblems you imagine? Uneven red, teal that doesn't
quite know what to do with itself, hesitant green
wanting to regress back to yellow. Even the gold
of the frame is tired and despondent.

Try to imagine what the frame doesn't hold:
an urban landscape with a misplaced state fairgrounds
and two lovers sweating into each other
in a nearby upper flat. In a week, the crack
house down the street will go up in flames.
In a month, two corpses will be carefully
arranged in the back alley. Next year,
a single bullet will find its way
into the lovers' kitchen. No questions
asked, no answers given. God just outside
your field of vision, with a closed mouth.

Counting Our Losses

—after a mixed media painting by Gary Elderidge

The questioning one:
silent heart, dried rose
fabric fraying at the edge.

The compliant two:
pacing the lines
of the forgotten poem.

The stubborn three:
the little bird who flew away
and never returned.

The perfect four:
infinite measure
of the diagram of your life.

The evasive five:
muted hand of regret
the old tree in the meadow.

The introverted six:
connected to the blank
window, the sash never opened.

The ascending seven:
not to heaven, nor the angel's
lowered eye, but to the infinite dark.

Eliminating the Horizon

—for Tom Andrews

Who needs boundaries?
If your eyes fail to imagine
where the earth ends and the sky
begins, think of a place bereft
of lines: the blue depths of a stream
flowing like hair that will never
be combed. Deep indigo of nothing
but fluid memory ebbing around
blossoms of white asters. "I remember
how flowers feel when you barely
touch them," says the water. Like leaving
one world and embracing another:
seeds bursting into wildflowers,
clouds changing into rain,
the image of our borders
a mere outline the soul ignores.

Contour of Absence

—after the painting "Provincetown in Winter, 1918"
by Gerrit Beneker

Is this what the new world has given us?
A place of broken ice, its center of negative
space devoid of real color except for the dreamlike
mauve, teal, and red of boats locked
and listing in their quiet sleep of winter.

Half-way into the continent, in a place of factories
not boats, my mother is being conceived
by her immigrant parents. Not for love
or passion or longing but to erase the contour
of absence: the silhouette of two daughters
who died the previous year. By illness
or accident, it makes no difference. The death
of a child releases one soul and enslaves
all others. The mother forgets to brush
her hair for weeks. The father can barely
remember how to walk down his street.

But how can my mother know this,
starting the thin journey to her life?
And how can the winter with all its snow and ice
mask true sorrow when everything
in this frozen universe hopes for spring?
The two boats leaning into each other
as if in unmarked graves. The sky,
gray and calm, waiting to be born.

Trinity

—after Magdalena Abakanowicz's
"Drawings: Cycle Corps"

I. Mother

You create your universe—a stone
of amber, layered with the past.
Fossilized bone, hint of birch leaf,
frozen delicacy of fly wing. Mother,
you trap the songs of birds
in your belly as if they're remnants
of a genesis story. Nightingale
and the birth of evening. Blue heron
and the color of the firmament. Gull
and the movement of the ocean. Owl
and the light of the stars. Hawk
and the language of rivers. Sparrow
and the first breath of man. Mourning dove
and the fullness of rest. No room
in this crowded universe for a mother's
lullaby. Only the sound of your heart
beyond the body that tries to contain it.

II. Daughter

I am hidden in the commonplace,
the ordinary, the face you never notice
in the mirror. I am at the crossroads
between idea and imagination where beauty
lies dormant and all lines converge
in disbelief or fervent prayer. No angel
announced my birth with silver-tipped wings,
gold-scented skin. I am only your shadow,
faint doppelgänger. The name you assume in dreams.

III. Spirit

Where light confides in darkness
where the circle grows its memory
where the trees reinvent history
where faceless men recognize each other
where sleepless women weave clouds
where their children name the constellations
where the sun braids the hair of comets
where the moon learns to write its name
where everything begins and nothing ends

Acknowledgments

Grateful acknowledgment is made to the editors of the following magazines and journals in which the following poems first appeared, some in slightly altered versions, and to ArtServe Michigan for an individual Creative Artist Grant that was instrumental in the completion of this book.

The Bonfire Review: "Sleeping in a Room Filled with the Past," "Tonight, No One is Safe"

The Bridge: "Groping" (published as "Groping in the Semi-Darkness at the Metropolitan Museum of Art")

The Chiron Review: "Copper Harbor: Early October" (published as "Copper Harbor, Michigan: Early October"), "The Nature of the Beast," "The Tao of Junk Mail," "Body Temple: The Teacher Addresses the Student"

Connecticut River Review: "A Sign from God"

Corridors: "Deserted Fairground, 1947"

The Driftwood Review: "The Gray Anatomy of the Crowd"

Dunes Review: "Counting Our Losses"

Eclipse: "Souvenir"

Ekphrasis: "The Son's Dream," "The Reinvention of Myth," "Trinity"

Free Lunch: "Piano Recital: Sonata with Mother and Child," "Forgotten Desire" (published as "Forgotten Desires")

Graffiti Rag: "Wild Pheasants in the City"

Great Midwestern Quarterly: "Birth"

Hiram Poetry Review: "In the Vicinity of Orion's Arm"

Korone: "Modern Landscape: Two Views of the World"

The MacGuffin: "Late Winter," "Her Obsession with Older Men," "The Blind and the Lame Swim at the 'Y'," "Eliminating the Horizon," "Contour of Absence," "Parasailing Above the Pacific"

The National Poetry Review: "The Field Behind the Dying Father's House"

Negative Capability: "The Third Secret of Fatima"

New American Writing: "Nativity Scene Encased in Saran Wrap"

New Millennium Writings: "Contrapuntal: Negative Space"

North American Review: "The Skin, The Blood: The Artists' Dialogue"

The Prose Poem: "False Spring: After Follain"

Quarterly West: "Village of the Mermaids: After Delvaux"

Rosebud: "Bad Art at the Clarkston Motor Inn"

Sou'wester: "Vision," "Paranoia for Two Voices"

Tendril: "Family Pose"

In the West of Ireland: "The Shape of Rain," "Total Eclipse" (published as "Total Eclipse of the Moon")

Word Wrights Magazine: "Holding the Air"

"Bad Art at the Clarkston Motor Inn" appeared in *The Best of Rosebud* (Eureka Productions)

"Climbing Cherry Trees" appeared in *With a Cherry on Top: Stories, Poems, Recipes & Fun Facts from Michigan Cherry Country* (Mayapple Press)

"The Third Secret of Fatima" appeared in *Contemporary Michigan Poetry: Poems from the Third Coast* (Wayne State University Press)

"Talking Diamonds" appeared in *Perceptions* (The Write Technique)

"Vision" appeared in *Places of Passage: Contemporary Catholic Poetry* (Story Line Press)

"Family Pose" appeared in *The Virago Book of Birth Poetry* (Virago Press)

Linda Nemec Foster has published thirteen collections of poetry, including *Bone Country* (Cornerstone Press), *The Blue Divide*, *Amber Necklace from Gdańsk*, and *The Lake Michigan Mermaid* (2019 Michigan Notable Book), which was created with co-author Anne-Marie Oomen and artist Meridith Ridl. Her work appears in magazines and journals such as *The Georgia Review*, *Nimrod*, *New American Writing*, *North American Review*, *Witness*, *Verse Daily*, and the *Best Small Fictions Anthology 2022*. She has received nominations for the Pushcart Prize and awards from the Arts Foundation of Michigan, National Writer's Voice, Dyer-Ives Foundation, The Poetry Center (NJ), *Fish Anthology* (Ireland), and the Academy of American Poets. The first Poet Laureate of Grand Rapids, Michigan (2003–2005), Foster is the founder of the Contemporary Writers Series at Aquinas College.